Christmas at Home

A SAMPLER OF CHRISTMAS WISDOM

WRITTEN AND COMPILED BY
ELLYN SANNA

BARBOUR
PUBLISHING, INC.
Uhrichsville, Ohio

Published by Barbour Publishing, Inc., P. O. Box 719, Uhrichsville, OH 44683
http://www.barbourbooks.com

 Member of the
Evangelical Christian
Publishers Association

Printed in Canada.

Table of Contents

1

Introduction:

The Wisdom of Christmas

*Now when Jesus was born in Bethlehem of Judaea
in the days of Herod the king, behold,
there came wise men from the east to Jerusalem,
Saying, Where is he that is born King of the Jews?
for we have seen his star in the east,
and are come to worship him.*

MATTHEW 2:1–2

Sometimes our world seems cold and dark and very foolish. We human beings allow little things to come between us; we seek our own way rather than the way of love; we allow material things, trivial things, to consume our lives.

And yet in the midst of all our foolish selfishness, the wisdom of Christmas shines like a star. Year after year, century after century, it offers the human race a glimpse of another way of doing things, a way that is heavenly and eternal, a way that centers on giving rather than taking, surrendering our own way to another rather than battling to the bitter end for our personal rights. In the midst of our tired, busy lives, Christmas teaches us of homecoming, of joy and celebration, of peace. It allows us to take a peek into a world beyond time, a world of eternal joy with God.

In short, Christmas shows us the true meaning of love.

Even our most worldly and commercialized Christmas celebrations still focus on giving. And so, despite the distractions of Santa Claus and shopping days, office parties and garish, blinking lights, Christmas still points our hearts toward the birthday of Love incarnate: Jesus Christ. He is the one who gave Himself to us completely; He is the Christmas Gift.

Like the wise men, we too may need to travel great distances in pursuit of the bright star we follow. We may get distracted on our journeys and turn aside. But the star shines patiently, undimmed by the darkness of our lives.

And once we allow the wisdom of Christmas to enter our hearts, we find we see things a little differently, not only at Christmas, but all year long.

I ask and wish not to appear
  More beauteous, rich, or gay:
Lord make me wiser every year,
  And better every day.

CHARLES LAMB

9

May we, like the wise men,
  follow the Christmas star. . . .

And by the light of that same Star,
Three Wise Men came from country far;
To seek for a King was their intent,
And to follow the star wherever it went.

This star drew nigh to the northwest,
O'er Bethlehem it took its rest;
And there it did both stop and stay,
Right over the place where Jesus lay.

Then entered in those Wise Men three,
Full reverently upon the knee,
And offered there, in His presence,
Their gold and myrrh and frankincense.

Then let us all with one accord,
Sing praises to our heavenly Lord;
That hath made heaven and earth of nought,
And with His blood mankind hath bought.

"THE FIRST NOEL," TRADITIONAL CAROL

What was it that made the wise men wise? What wisdom did they demonstrate?

• The wise men noticed the sign that pointed to Christ's coming. They were not too preoccupied, too busy with the details of their lives to see that which no one else even noticed.

Show me, Lord, where Your light glimmers in my life. Help me not be so busy, so rushed, that I hurry past, without ever noticing the signs of Your coming.

- When the wise men saw the star that pointed to Christ's birth, they committed their lives to finding out more. They could have talked and wondered about the star their whole lives, without ever knowing anything more about it—but instead, they allowed it to change the shape and reality of how they lived. Instead of being rich, pampered kings, they became travelers, pilgrims into the unknown.

Give me strength, dear Jesus, to follow You. . .even when I don't know where I'm going. When the way is dark and long, may I still follow Your light.

- The wise men recognized Jesus when they saw Him. When they found a poor Child born to humble parents, they might have gone right on searching for the king they had imagined, never knowing they had found Him. But instead, as soon as they saw Him, they were filled with joy. And they fell down and worshipped Him.

My Lord, please empty my mind of all my preconceived notions about what You should look like. Help me to grasp Your true reality, so that I may be filled with Your joy. I worship You, Lord Jesus.

• They opened their treasure chests and gave Jesus gifts.

Jesus, my life's treasure chest seems so empty sometimes. Help me to lay at Your feet all the things to which I cling, no matter how small or broken they may be. Thank You for accepting my gifts. You gave everything at Christmas—may I be wise enough to give You my all in return.

Some people are hard to shop for at Christmas—
but Jesus is not one of them.
He simply wants us to give Him whatever we have:
our joys, our heartaches, our love. . .

Can we see the little Child,
Is He within?
If we lift the wooden latch
May we go in?

Great kings have precious gifts,
And we have nought,
Little smiles and little tears
Are all we brought.

FRANCES CHESTERTON

O. Henry's short story "The Gift of the Magi" tells of a young wife who sells her beautiful, long hair so she can buy her husband a watch fob for a Christmas gift. . .and her husband who sells his watch so he can buy an ornament for his wife's beautiful, long hair. Despite the irony, their gifts are nevertheless wise ones, because the husband and wife give themselves away. . . .

The magi, as you know, were wise men—wonderfully wise men who brought gifts to the Babe in the manger. They invented the art of giving Christmas presents. Being wise, their gifts were no doubt wise ones, possibly bearing the privilege of exchange in case of duplication. And here I have lamely related to you the uneventful chronicle of two foolish children in a flat who most unwisely sacrificed for each other the greatest treasures of their house. But in a last word to the wise of these days let it be said that of all who give gifts these two were the wisest. Of all who give and receive gifts, such as they are wisest. Everywhere they are wisest. They are the magi.

O. HENRY

Christmas Choice

"In the beginning God created. . ."
Human beings, and He gave us freedom of choice.
This Christmas I am free to choose my heart attitude.

The biblical account gives me many examples:
Angels proclaimed the Good News;
Shepherds were amazed and ran to Him;

Wise men sought Him with exceeding joy,
  Following a star that lit their way until they reached Him,
  And then they presented their gifts and worshipped Him.
Meanwhile, Herod was troubled,
Joseph, not seeking to understand, simply obeyed God;
And Mary treasured all these things, pondering them in her heart.

Which will I do?

MARTHA O. GIRTON

This Christmas, Lord, help me to pursue the true wisdom of Christmas as faithfully as the wise men followed the star. May its light guide me through all the busy days; may it brighten every family celebration; may it strengthen our love for each other and put peace in our hearts. No matter how hectic my Christmas schedule this year, Lord, may I be like Mary, who quietly treasured You in her heart. Amen.

2

Rest for Our Hearts:

A Time for Homecoming

And I do come home for Christmas.
We all do, or we all should.
We all come home, or ought to come home,
for a short holiday—
the longer, the better. . .
to take, and give a rest.

CHARLES DICKENS

$\mathcal{A}$nd numerous indeed are the hearts to which Christmas brings a brief season of happiness and enjoyment. How many families whose members have been dispersed and scattered far and wide, in the restless struggle of life, are then reunited, and meet once again in that happy state of companionship and mutual goodwill, which is a source of such pure and unalloyed delight, and one so incompatible with the cares and sorrows of the world that the religious belief of the most civilized nations, and the rude traditions of the roughest savages, alike number it among the first days of a future state of existence, provided for the blest and happy!

WASHINGTON IRVING

At Christmastime, our hearts turn home. We long for the familiar scent of our mother's baking; we anticipate being with the people we love the most; we look forward to the old traditions we remember from our childhoods. In a restless world of change, Christmas is like an oasis of stability, a place where we can rest our hearts.

Sometimes the best part about going home for Christmas is just sitting around the table talking. . . .

Love comes from the heart and can best be made known by language. Grandma Mollie, with an Irishwoman's belief that we exist more fully when we let others know by the words we use what lies at our heart's core, initiated Christmas afternoons of talk. The talk could be spontaneous; could be the repetition of a poet's words; could be one's memory of words spoken by a forebear long departed the world. Whatever it was, it revealed our hearts.

JESSAMYN WEST

C hristmas is a time of love and welcome, a time of security. But we need not go home geographically to find that sense of total safety.

Joyful times with our extended families are a wonderful part of Christmas. That moment when we pull into the familiar driveway and the front door is flung open before we're even out of the car. . .well, for me, that's one of the best moments of the entire Christmas season. Between hugs, we struggle to carry in bags of gifts, while everyone talks at once in a happy jumble of unfinished questions and answers about the trip, and the meal, and who will be arriving next.

But the true meaning of Christmas homecomings does not depend on a particular place or even particular people, for the warmth of our earthly homes is a mere reflection of our heavenly home with Jesus. No matter where we are, no matter how far in years and miles from the people we love, our hearts can still go home at Christmas.

All we have to do is turn to Jesus, and He will give us love and welcome, security and rest.

*M*y childhood home was not always a happy place. And yet Christmas was a good time. Now, as an adult, each year at Christmas I look back at my home and catch a glimpse of what it could have been, had all our days centered on Christ. He was there with me, shining in the Christmas tree lights, wrapped up in the presents, warming our unhappy house into a home. These days I may not go home for Christmas physically—but each year, while all my friends pack their bags and plan their holiday homecomings, inside my heart I hurry home anew to Jesus.

LUCIE CHRISTOPHER

A Homesick Heart

"I want to go home," the old woman whimpered. She huddled on her bed, rocking herself back and forth, like a lost child.

Becky looked at her doubtfully. This was her first day working as an aide in the nursing home, and she wasn't sure what she should do. She had mentioned to her supervisor that Mrs. Brown seemed upset, but her supervisor had merely sighed and shaken her head. "She's always upset, Becky. Don't worry about her. There's nothing we can do for her."

Becky's shift was over, and she was eager to punch out and go home. By the time she got there, her older brother would be back from college for his Christmas break.

Her mother would have trays of cookies waiting, a fire would be crackling in the fireplace, and Becky could take her shoes off her tired feet and collapse beside the Christmas tree. . . .

But the loneliness in Mrs. Brown's voice hurt Becky's heart. She couldn't walk away and leave her. It would be like turning her back on a frightened child.

Becky thought of her baby niece who often cried for her mother when Becky was caring for her. Becky had learned the best way to deal with her niece's tears was to simply distract her.

She couldn't give her what she really wanted, but she could get her to think about something else. Maybe the same principle would work with Mrs. Brown.

"Come on." She gently pulled Mrs. Brown to her feet. "Come for a walk with me."

Mrs. Brown shuffled along the corridor beside her. Her tears subsided, but her face was still anxious. "I want to go home," she whispered. Her hands twisted her pink housecoat again and again. "Please, can't I just go home?"

Becky knew Mrs. Brown's home had long ago been sold; she had been a resident in the nursing home for the past six years.

Blinking away her own tears, Becky put an arm around Mrs. Brown's shoulders. "Come here," she said softly. "I'll show you something pretty."

The overhead light was turned off in the common room, but Becky knew the tall Christmas tree was glowing softly in the corner. She hoped the lights would interest Mrs. Brown the way they did her niece, and so she guided Mrs. Brown through the doorway.

Mrs. Brown stood still. As she looked at the Christmas tree, her face lit up with joy. She held out her frail, trembling hands as though she wanted to catch the light and grasp it tight. "Home," she breathed. She turned to Becky and hugged her. "You brought me home."

O come, O come, Emmanuel,
And ransom captive Israel,
That mourns in lonely exile here
Until the Son of God appear.

Rejoice! Rejoice! Emmanuel
Shall come to thee, O Israel.

LATIN HYMN

I thank Thee, O Lord God, that though with liberal hand Thou hast at all times showered Thy blessing upon our human kind, yet in Jesus Christ Thou hast done greater things for us than Thou ever didst before:

- *Making home sweeter and friends dearer*
- *Turning sorrow into gladness and pain into the soul's victory...*

Amen.

JOHN BAILLIE

*L*ord,

Thank You for our homes. Thank You for people who love us, for places where we can go to rest, for times to simply be together with our families.

But even more, Lord, we thank You for throwing open the doors of heaven, welcoming us to a place of eternal rest and joy and love. Thank You for coming to our earth so we can all go home to You. Amen.

3

The Dwelling Place of Eternity:
A Time of Peace

Peace was the first thing the angels sang.
Peace is the mark of the sons of God.
Peace is the nurse of love.
Peace is the mother of unity.
Peace is the rest of blessed souls.
Peace is the dwelling place of eternity.

LEO THE GREAT

*Peace comes when
there is no cloud between us and God.*

CHARLES H. BRENT

*Hark! The herald angels sing,
"Glory to the newborn King;
Peace on earth, and mercy mild,
God and sinners reconciled!"*

CHARLES WESLEY
ALTERED BY GEORGE WHITEFIELD

In our war-filled world, we hear a lot about peace. Peace is elusive, though; no matter how we strive to grab hold of it, it continues to slip away. Just as one war is resolved, another breaks out. It seems unlikely this world can ever achieve lasting and permanent peace.

But despite the turmoil in our world, peace is not beyond our grasp. True peace, peace of heart, comes to us when nothing separates us from God. Christmas marks the birth of the Prince of Peace into our world. Jesus is the bridge that crosses any chasm; He is the door through any wall; He is the way through any maze, no matter how puzzling. Through Jesus, we are no longer separated from God. This is the peace of Christmas.

He has come! the Prince of Peace;
Come to bid our sorrows cease;
Come to scatter with His light
All the darkness of our night.

Unto us a Son is given!
He has come from God's own heaven,
Bringing with Him, from above,
Holy peace and holy love.

HORATIUS BONAR

$\mathcal{P}$eace is God's free gift to us through Christ. But we need to intentionally plan how we will keep the peace of Christmas alive in our hearts all year round. . . .

Prayerful planning is an attitude of caring about the Christmas story, of feeling its significance for the twentieth century, and of being sensitive to how this is shared with family and friends. Prayerful planning guides celebrants in searching for the true meaning of Christmas. Just as the wise men returned home by a different route after seeing Jesus (Matthew 2:12), our annual journeys to Bethlehem can guide us back to our jobs, schools, and homes along different routes than we previously traveled. Christmas becomes a time of renewal.

HARVEY COX

$\mathcal{H}$*e is the happiest,*
be he king or peasant,
who finds peace in his home.

JOHANN WOLFGANG VON GOETHE

We can miss the peace Christmas offers us by cramming too many activities into the month of December. Instead of resting at the feet of the Prince of Peace, like Mary of Bethany did, we become like her sister Martha, burdened and fretful with too many responsibilities. Sometimes, we become so nearsighted we perceive the items on our detailed to-do lists as necessities rather than options: We *have* to bake twelve dozen cookies; we *have* to have an eight-foot Christmas tree perfectly decorated in a manner worthy of a magazine cover; we *have* to send two hundred greeting cards; and we *have* to host three family get-togethers, one holiday party, and provide the refreshments for two Christmas functions at church.

But the truth of the matter is this: We *do* have a choice. The Prince of Peace will be born into our lives, quietly, simply, certainly, regardless of whether we check even one item off our to-do lists. And if we choose to sit quietly in His presence, leaving some of our many responsibilities undone, we will find that we sense His coming that much more clearly.

It is of great importance that you endeavour, at all times, to keep your hearts in peace; that you may keep pure that temple of God. The way to keep it in peace is to enter into it by means of inward silence. When you see yourself more sharply assaulted, retreat into that region of peace; and you will find a fortress that will enable you to triumph over all your enemies, visible and invisible, and over all their snares and temptations.

WILLIAM BACKHOUSE AND JAMES JANSEN,
A Guide to True Peace

A New Tradition

As we joined the ranks of "empty nesters" and moved into a small row house, we had not fully anticipated what the space limitations would involve. The living room was narrow, with a single recessed window. A small dining room/kitchen area was the only other room on the first floor.

We were adjusting well, however. We even managed to make room for the piano. Then the holidays approached. Where could we possibly put the tree?

Like most families, we had our traditions. Christmas just wouldn't seem complete without them, we thought—and a large tree adorned with hundreds of ornaments was a central part of our traditional Christmas.

Those ornaments had been used for generations. They evoked precious memories of Christmases past and the loving people who had shared them. We were reluctant to give up those memories and traditions. But really, we simply had no room for a big tree. What could we do?

My eye fell on the recessed front window. I realized the two-foot nook would accommodate a small, narrow tree. In the window like that, the tree would not only decorate our living room, but it would be visible to all who passed by as well. With a sense of resignation, I began to look for a tree with the proper shape.

We found a live tree, just the right size, with balled roots; as an added bonus, we could plant it outside after the holidays. I discovered I was becoming more satisfied, even excited, with our decision.

But the next challenge was deciding which of our many cherished ornaments we should hang on our small tree. One by one, we took them out of their boxes, and one by one we eliminated them; they were just too large for such a small tree.

At last, the only thing left in the box was a small crèche, complete with shepherds, animals, wise men, and two angels. With a sigh, I placed the crèche under the tree and put the two angels just above it on a tree limb. When I stood back to look at the effect, I had an immediate vision for the little tree.

We went shopping for small angels in a variety of styles. Back home, we spaced them carefully among the tree's branches. Then we added a few little white lights and a lit star at the very top. Garlands of gold stars hung suspended above the tree, sparkling

as the breeze from the ceiling fan gently moved them. We surveyed the finished scene with satisfaction. Our simple decoration, with its stars and angels, and most of all, its manger, was a tangible reminder of the first Christmas.

All through the season, our little tree kept our focus on the "reason for the season." In the midst of all the holiday hustle and bustle, whenever I looked at our tree I felt a sense of calm assurance.

With the arrival of the new year, we reluctantly packed away the crèche, the angels, the lights, and the stars in their own special boxes, where they would await the next Christmas, and the next, and the next. We'd made a new tradition, I realized. A tradition that will always remind me that the peace and joy of Christmas does not depend on any decoration, no matter how

cherished, nor on any human tradition, no matter how lovely.

The peace of Christmas depends only on that long-ago crèche, with its shepherds and wise men, angels and stars. But all we really need is the Baby.

MARTHA O. GIRTON

To thee, O God, we turn for peace;
but grant us, too,
the blessed assurance that nothing shall
deprive us of that peace,
neither ourselves, nor our foolish, earthly desires,
nor my wild longings,
nor the anxious cravings of my heart.

SOREN KIERKEGAARD

Peace does not mean the end of all our striving,
Joy does not mean the drying of our tears.
Peace is the power that comes to souls arriving
Up to the light where God Himself appears.

G. A. Studdert-Kennedy

*D*ear Lord,
Fill our hearts this year with Your peace. In the midst of all the busy celebrations, may we never lose sight of Your face. Allow us to take Your peace with us as we head into the new year.

Lord, we want nothing to come between You and us, for we long to dwell with You in eternity. Amen.

4

The Evergreen of Life:

A Time for Merriness

*Laughter is the
joyous universal evergreen of life.*

ABRAHAM LINCOLN

We don't use the word "merry" much anymore, only in connection with Christmas. In our serious, care-worn world, sometimes the hysterical laughter of sitcoms is the only relief we find from the somberness of daily existence.

But I don't think that's the way God wants it. He wants our hearts to be merry, full of laughter and plain old, innocent silliness. As we sit around the tree late on Christmas Eve, laughing with our families over everything and nothing, I believe God laughs with us. He's delighted by our fun—our merriness, if you will.

We're used to thinking of the Incarnation in terms of pain and suffering. But maybe one reason Jesus came is simply because He wanted us to have fun again, free from the cloud of sin, the way Adam and Eve must have enjoyed themselves in the Garden.

And maybe when we get to heaven, we'll find that what looked like childish silliness here on earth is really part of the serious, joyful business of eternity.

Because the foolishness of God is wiser than men. . .
1 CORINTHIANS 1:25

$\mathcal{D}$ance and game are frivolous,
unimportant down here;
for "down here" is not their natural place.
Here, they are a moment's rest from
the life we were placed here to live.
But in this world everything is upside down.

C. S. LEWIS

$\mathcal{D}$eck the halls with boughs of holly,
'Tis the season to be jolly,
Don we now our gay apparel,
Troll the ancient Yuletide carol.

See the blazing Yule before us,
Strike the harp and join the chorus,
Follow me in merry measure,
While I tell of Yuletide treasure.

Welsh Traditional Carol

But cold and selfish should we be,
And heartless, did we fail
To wish that you as well as we,
May merry be and hale!
May He whose love has ever blest
The righteous with its ray,
Grant you all good—and 'midst the rest
A merry Christmas Day!

ANONYMOUS

Wise Silliness

Our family has an odd Christmas tradition. I don't know how it started—but every year, after we've unwrapped all the gifts, and the floor is strewn with paper and ribbons, the children bury Aunt Lillian.

Down on the floor she goes, my seventy-something-year-old aunt, while her great nieces and great nephews leap to their feet and hurl paper over her with wild abandon. Soon all we can see is a great mound of crumpled paper with a few tangled ribbons on top. The children step back, holding their breaths. . .

The paper moves. A single finger reaches out, then a hand, then an arm. . . The children shriek and fling more paper to cover

the hand—and then the foot that sticks out—and then the few gray curls that peek out among the gaily printed paper. No matter how hard they try, though, they can't seem to keep her covered. They laugh until they can barely breathe.

At last, when the children are exhausted (and Aunt Lillian, too, no doubt), the activity subsides. We adults shake our heads and pick up the mess. Someone helps Aunt Lillian to her feet. With a wistful sigh that the game is over for another year, the children go back to their seats.

"I don't think Aunt Lillian will ever get old," my niece whispered in my ear one year. "She's too silly."

I smiled and nodded. I hope I, too, can be as young when I am seventy-something.

He saw that men who worked h[...] scanty bread with lives of labour, we[...] that to the most ignorant, the sweet face [...] failing source of cheerfulness and joy. He saw those [...] icately nurtured, and tenderly brought up, cheerful under [...] and superior to suffering that would have crushed many of a rou[...] grain, because they bore within their own bosoms the materials of happiness, contentment, and peace. . .that women, the tenderest and most fragile of all God's creatures, were the oftenest superior to sorrow,

adversity, and distress; and he saw that it was because they bore, in their own hearts, an inexhaustible wellspring of ...ection and devotion. Above all, he saw that men like himself, who ...narled at the mirth and cheerfulness of others, were the foulest weeds on the fair surface of the earth; and setting all the good of the world against the evil, he came to the conclusion that it was a very decent and respectable sort of world after all.

CHARLES DICKENS

Festivity then is a time set aside
for the full expression of feeling.
It says yes to experience;
it entails joy,
which explains why we wish people
happiness on holidays.

HARVEY COX

A Merry Heart

Sometimes, as an adult, I forget how to play and be silly. My life is full of worries and serious duties, and I'm all too aware of the presence of pain and hardship in the world. The merriness of Christmas seems frivolous and immature. But sometimes I suspect I've simply forgotten how to enjoy the moment with a child's wholehearted abandon.

I've formed the habit of always longing for something I don't have. *Oh, if only I were done with this work project,* I think to myself, *then I would be happy.* Or I think, *Oh, if only we had a bigger house,* or *if only we could pay off all our debts.* The things I long for may be well and good in themselves. . .but by focusing on what I don't have yet, I miss the simple innocent pleasures each day offers. Like the little tree in Hans Christian Andersen's story "The Little Fir Tree," I long for a life anywhere but where I am at the moment.

In Andersen's story, when the little fir tree was in the woods, he wanted to be sent on a ship across the sea. Then he longed to be cut and taken in at Christmas. The words of the tree reflect the discontent I so often allow to take root in my own life: "Were I in the warm room with all the splendor and magnificence! Yes; then something better, something still grander, will surely follow. . . . Oh, how I long, how I suffer! I do not know myself what is the matter with me!"

"Rejoice in our presence!" the Air and the Sunlight tell him. But the little fir tree does not listen to them. Even when he gets his wish and is taken inside to be a Christmas tree, he continues to wait for something grander, unable to find the delight of the moment, until he is carted away to the attic. When the family comes to clear out the attic, the tree says to himself: "Now a merry life will begin again," and "Now, then, I shall really enjoy life." But when he sees in the bright light of day how yellowed and withered he is, he wishes he could have remained in the attic. The story closes with the tree lamenting: " 'Tis over! 'Tis past! Had I but rejoiced when I had reason to do so! But now 'tis past, 'tis past!"

"Do you remember how to play?" one of my children asked me recently.

"Of course I do," I answered, but she looked at me doubtfully, with a hint of pity in her eyes. Suddenly, I felt ashamed.

I love what I do, I wanted to say to her. *I love being with you children and with your father; I love making books. For me those things are like playing.* And sometimes that's true. But sometimes I get obsessed with responsibilities and accomplishments; the truth of the matter is that most of the time I'm simply far too busy to play. *Later,* I say to myself, *when I get this done, when we get that bill paid, when I get the house organized, when I accomplish this, when I achieve that. . . .*

I don't want to be like the little fir tree, always longing for something I don't have. I want to be like a child, delighting in all the pure moments of silly fun that God sprinkles through my day. I want to remember how to play. And I want to have a merry heart not only at Christmastime, but all year round.

If only we—like Jesus—
would take the time to listen to,
share with, and enjoy those around us!
If only we would stop waiting for the "right time"
and celebrate the "right-now time!" . . .
A true *celebration fills the premises with joy.*

HARVEY COX

$\mathcal{D}$*ear Lord,*
Make us free by the power of Your Spirit—so that we can play again like children. May we truly have a merry Christmas. Amen.

5

Entertaining Angels:

A Time of Hospitality and Goodwill

*B*e not forgetful to entertain strangers:
for thereby some have entertained angels unawares.

HEBREWS 13:2

*L*et every heart prepare Him room,
And heav'n and nature sing.

ISAAC WATTS

On the very first Christmas, heaven flung its doors wide open, and the angels rushed out with a song of welcome and goodwill. As human beings, stumbling along in our shadowy little world, we nevertheless echo the angels' song whenever we turn to one another and open the doors of our hearts and homes. As heaven and nature sing at Christmas time, let us be sure to prepare room in our hearts, both for Jesus and for each other.

*To make some nook of God's Creation
a little fruitfuller, better, more worthy of God;
to make some human hearts a little wiser,
manfuller, happier—more blessed, less accursed!
It is work for a God.*

THOMAS CARLYLE

The example [Christ] set is still before us, and His attitude can be ours as well. "Wherever two or three are gathered in my name, there am I in the midst of them," He said (Matthew 18:20). As we gather to share in the spirit of love that is Christmas, we can be assured that Jesus is with us and that His caring is ours to share.

HARVEY COX

Christmas turns things tail end foremost. The day and the spirit of Christmas rearrange the world parade. As the world arranges it, usually there come first in importance—leading the parade with a big blare of a band—the Big Shots. Frequently they are also the Stuffed Shirts. That's the first of the parade. Then at the tail end, as of little importance, trudge the weary, the poor, the lame, the halt, and the blind. But in the Christmas spirit, the procession is turned around. Those at the tail end are put first in the arrangement of the Child of Christmas.

HALFORD E. LUCCOCK

$\mathcal{F}$olk tales from around the world tell of poor, simple folk who unknowingly welcomed the Christ Child, while those with greater wealth turned Him away. At Christmastime—and all year long—let us reach out to those in need. Whenever we make time for a lonely neighbor, whenever we share our wealth with children in other countries, whenever we send our winter coats to those in our community who would otherwise do without, we, too, are welcoming the Christ Child into our lives.

And like the simple folk in all the stories, we, too, will be blessed.

Inasmuch as ye have done it unto one of the least of these my brethren, ye have done it unto me.
MATTHEW 25:40

When compassion for the common man was born on Christmas Day, with it was born new hope among the multitudes. They feel a great, ever-rising determination to lift themselves and their children out of hunger and disease and misery, up to a higher level. Jesus started a fire upon the earth, and it is burning hot today, the fire of a new hope in the hearts of the hungry multitudes.

FRANK C. LAUBACH

Nothing is so easy to men of goodwill as goodwill itself, and this is all that God requires. Every act of goodwill permanently and sensibly increases goodwill. Trifling acts of goodwill are often more efficacious in this way than great ones. A flower given in kindness and at the right time profits more, both to giver and receiver, than some vast material benefit in which the goodwill is hidden by the magnitude of the act. Some little, sensible, individual touch from the hand of our Lord may convert the heart more than the contemplation of His death for us.

COVENTRY PATMORE

How shall we love Thee, holy hidden Being,
If we love not the world which Thou hast made?
O give us brother-love for better seeing
Thy Word made flesh, and in a manger laid.

LAURENCE HOUSMAN

Voices in the Mist

The time draws near the birth of Christ:
The moon is hid; the night is still:
The Christmas bells from hill to hill
Answer each other in the mist.

Each voice changes on the wind,
That now dilate, and now decrease,
Peace and goodwill, goodwill and peace,
Peace and goodwill, to all mankind.

ALFRED LORD TENNYSON

$\mathcal{D}$ear Lord,
This year at Christmas may we open our hearts wide to those around us—and may we keep them open all year round. Remind us that we cannot turn to You while we turn away from those around us. Fill us with the goodwill and hospitality of the true Christmas spirit. Amen.

6

Small Gifts:

A Time of Joy

The smallest things become great when
God requires them of us;
they are small only in themselves;
they are always great when they are done for God,
and when they serve to unite us
with Him eternally.

FRANCOIS FÉNELON

$\mathcal{T}$he small intimate gestures of friends and loved ones are sometimes the best gifts of all. . . .

These are the gifts that warm me, make me feel wanted, show me that in the meaning of another's life I have meaning. . . . These small gifts, these almost offhanded, throwaway spontaneous things are what fill me with a mighty joy.

KAREN BURTON MAINS

Joy to the world! the Lord is come!
Let earth receive her King. . . .
Joyful all ye nations rise,
Join the triumph of the skies;
With th' angelic host proclaim
Christ is born in Bethlehem.

ISAAC WATTS

A Child's Understanding

"I think I know what our best gifts were this year," my six-year-old daughter told me on Christmas night.

"What's that?" I asked as I leaned down to tuck her in. I expected her to say the new dolls her grandmother gave her and her sister, or maybe the new computer game from their uncle.

"All the hugs." She rubbed her eyes. "Those were the best gifts."

"Why do you think?" I asked, surprised.

She shook her head sleepily, as though she knew I knew better.

"Because the hugs say *I love you*, Mommy. And that's what makes us really happy." She rolled over and buried her nose in her blankets, leaving me to stand a moment longer in her quiet room, wondering at her wisdom.

The world is so full of a number of things,
I'm sure we should all be as happy as kings.

ROBERT LOUIS STEVENSON

Children know that the world is full of tiny, amazing gifts, not just at Christmas but all the time. Day after day at breakfast, my children are entranced by the way the light breaks in rainbow streaks through the prisms that hang in our kitchen window. Over and over, they gaze in wonder at the infinitesimal crystalline shapes of snowflakes on their mittens. They're never too busy; they never seem to tire of seeing the bits of loveliness scattered through our lives. With their sharp, fresh eyes, they see joy everywhere.

As adults, sometimes our vision is clouded with hurt and weariness and worry. But those small, joyous gifts are still there, offered to us by a loving Father who delights in our pleasure. All we have to do is open our eyes and look.

Sometimes we adults miss the tiny joys God gives us. We look at things in terms of our own convenience, rather than with a child's wondering vision. As a result, we see December's snow and ice and cold merely in terms of slippery roads to hinder our holiday traveling, driveways to shovel when we're too busy, and high heating bills at the same time we're paying for Christmas gifts.

But children are wiser than we are. They know that snow and ice and cold are magic. . . .

A Jewel Day

O Children, wake, for a fairy world
Is waiting for you and me,
With gems aglow on the meadow grass,
And jewels on every tree.

The hedgerows glitter, the dark woods shine
In dresses of sparkling white,
For while we slumbered, the Ice Queen passed
All over the earth last night.

LUCY DIAMOND

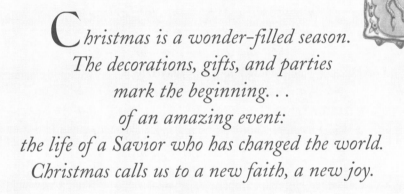

Christmas is a wonder-filled season.
The decorations, gifts, and parties
mark the beginning. . .
of an amazing event:
the life of a Savior who has changed the world.
Christmas calls us to a new faith, a new joy.

HARVEY COX

Hear we no beat of drums, fanfare, nor cry,
When Christ the herald comes quietly nigh;
Splendor He makes on earth;
Color awakes on earth;
Suddenly breaks on earth light from the sky.
Bid then farewell to sleep: rise up and run!
What though the hill be steep? Strength's in the sun.
Now you shall find at last
Night's left behind at last,
And for mankind at last, Day has begun!

JAN STRUTHER

D*ear Lord,*
May Christmas sharpen our eyes. Remind us to see the small gifts of
joy You offer us every day. Amen.

7

The Revelation of God:
A Time for Love

No, no other holiday,
is comparable to the day when
wise men and shepherds followed
the shine of a star which led them to a crib
where they learned that God is love.
We still believe it.
And on Christmas Day we try to practice it.

JESSAMYN WEST

True Christmas wisdom can be summed up best by one word: love. Christmas is the demonstration of God's love for us through Jesus. This year at Christmas, let us demonstrate our love for Him.

A scientist said,
making a plea for exchange scholarships
between nations,
"The very best way to send an idea is
to wrap it up in a person."
That was what happened at Christmas.
The idea of divine love was wrapped up in a Person.

HALFORD E. LUCCOCK

The Second Person in God, the Son, became human Himself: was born into the world as an actual man—a real man of a particular height, with hair of a particular color, speaking a particular language, weighing so many stone. The Eternal Being, who knows everything and created the whole universe, became not only a man but (before that) a baby, and before that fetus inside a Woman's body.

C. S. LEWIS

Jesus Christ was born:
Born in a stable,
Cradled in a manger,
In the world His hands had made,
Born a stranger.

CHRISTINA ROSSETTI

Sometimes at Christmas we are filled with a sentimental longing for childhood's magic and wonder. But perhaps what we are really longing for after all is not some lost quality of innocence we can never hope to regain as adults. Instead, our hearts may be filled with yearning for Something as real today as when we were children—Jesus Christ, the Baby born at Christmas who lives eternally.

$\mathfrak{T}$he sentimentality that I felt at Christmas was not just for the times of youth and happiness with family and friends long gone, but for the sure anchor of faith that I had let go of.

The intervening years for me have been a process of retracing those steps that led me away from Christ. In recovering faith and belief, I have recovered much more than the retrieval of a lost childhood could ever mean: I have rediscovered the Child Who became the Savior. And

so, at last, I can celebrate Christmas without the wistful sense that it is, after all, just a story. Indeed, for me, it is now THE story, the story of how my hope was born, the story of how my despair was lifted, the story of how it all began for me, the story of each of us, the true story.

ROBERT McANALLY ADAMS

*Advent is a matter of
looking for Christ-comings,
of getting ready to mark nativity as it peeks
through in small ways today, and today.
And today. . .
Christ is amassed all the year in these epiphanies,
in these common showings made uncommon,
in the power of the everyday unmasked.*

KAREN BURTON MAINS

"I know what love would look like if you could see it," my daughter said to me.

"What?" I asked, wondering what her odd little mind had come up with this time.

"Like Jesus," she said with assurance. " 'Cause Jesus is love with bones and hair."

Bright portals of the sky,
Emboss'd with sparkling stars,
Doors of eternity,
With diamantine bars,
Your arras rich uphold,
Loose all your bolts and springs,
Ope wide your leaves of gold,
That in your roofs may come the King of Kings.

O glory of the heaven!
O sole delight of earth!
To thee all power be given,
God's uncreated birth!
Of mankind lover true,
Indearer of his wrong,
Who doth the world renew,
Still be thou our salvation and our song!

WILLIAM DRUMMOND

Our God, heav'n cannot hold Him
Nor earth sustain;
Heav'n and earth shall flee away
When He comes to reign:

In the bleak mid-winter
A stable place sufficed
The Lord God Almighty
Jesus Christ

Enough for Him, whom cherubim
Worship night and day,
A breastful of milk
And a mangerful of hay;

Enough for Him, whom angels
Fall down before,
The ox and ass and camel
Which adore.

CHRISTINA ROSSETTI

The Arms of God

My first-grader was all Christmased out. She was exhausted and whiney and not very pleasant to have around. At last, I sent her upstairs to her room, knowing what she needed more than anything else was a nap. A few minutes later, though, she came trailing down the stairs again, her woebegone face streaked with tears.

"What do you want now?" I asked her, exasperated.

She climbed onto my lap. "This," she said with an exhausted

sigh as I wrapped my arms around her. "I just needed to feel you so I'd know you still love me."

God always loves us. But like tired children, sometimes we're so worn out we no longer experience His presence. God is too big, too awesome, too far beyond our abilities to comprehend—and so from our tiny, limited perspective, we assume He's too far-away and distant to really love us.

Maybe that's one reason He sent us His Son to be one of us. He wanted to communicate Himself in a way we would understand. He wanted to give us Someone whose arms we could feel.

The King of glory sends His Son,
To make His entrance on this earth;
Behold the midnight bright as noon,
And heav'nly hosts declare His birth!
About the young Redeemer's head,
What wonders, and what glories meet!
An unknown star arose, and led
The eastern sages to His feet.

Simeon and Anna both conspire
The infant Saviour to proclaim;
Inward they felt the sacred fire,
And bless'd the babe, and own'd His name.
Let pagan hordes blaspheme aloud,
And treat the holy child with scorn;
Our souls adore th' eternal God
Who condescended to be born.

ISAAC WATTS

Jesus came!—and came for me.
Simple words! and yet expressing
Depths of holy mystery,
Depths of wondrous love and blessing.
Holy Spirit, make me see
All His coming means for me;
Take the things of Christ, I pray,
Show them to my heart today.

FRANCES RIDLEY HAVERGAL

As a mother, whenever I held my newborn babies in my arms, I would be struck by their total and absolute vulnerability. Human newborns are overwhelmingly, awesomely dependent on their parents for care. My responsibility to them as their mother was intensely sweet and intensely frightening.

Imagine, then, how Mary must have felt as she held the Creator of the universe, clothed in swaddling clothes. How did God dare to send His only Son in such a terrifyingly fragile package?

Come worship the King,
That little dear thing,
Asleep on His Mother's soft breast.
Ye bright stars, bow down,
Weave for Him a crown,
Christ Jesus by angels confessed.
Come, children, and peep,
But hush ye, and creep
On tiptoe to where the Babe lies;
Then whisper His Name
And lo! like a flame
The glory light shines in His eyes.

Come strong men, and see
This high mystery,
Tread firm where the shepherds have trod,
And watch, 'mid the hair
Of the Maiden so fair,
The five little fingers of God.
Come, old men and grey,
The star leads the way,
It halts and your wanderings cease;
Look down on His Face
Then, filled with His Grace,
Depart ye, God's servants, in Peace.

G. A. STUDDERT-KENNEDY

G*iven, not lent,*
And not withdrawn, once sent,
This Infant of mankind, this One,
Is still the little welcome Son.
New every year,
New-born and newly dear,
He comes with tidings and a song,
The ages long, the ages long.

Even as the cold
Keen winter grows not old,
As childhood is so fresh, forseen,
And spring in the familiar green.
Sudden as sweet
Come the expected feet.
All joy is young, and new all art,
And He, too, whom we have by heart.

ALICE MAYNELL

122

God's Vulnerability

And the Word was made flesh,
and dwelt among us.
JOHN 1:14

God, incarnated in Jesus, gives Himself to us not only at a particular point in history, at Christmas, but always and forever.

How do we understand this? How is it played out? What does it mean?

- *It means* we have a God who chose to limit Himself, restrict Himself, by becoming involved in the human condition.

- *It means* we have a God who suffers when we suffer, thirsts when we thirst.

- *It means* we have a God who now depends on us to be His feet, His hands, His eyes, in a world forever absorbed in compulsive egocentrism.

- *It means* we have a God who granted us freedom at the risk of becoming an unrequited Lover.

- *It means* we have a God whose longing for us far exceeds our longing for Him, whose desire for us far exceeds our desire for Him.

- *It means* we have a God who knows only too well our deceit, our shame, our brutality, but who, nevertheless, works all things for good.

- *It means* we have a God who is forever courteous, never forcing Himself upon us but rather nudging us, coaxing us, to turn our lives around.

- *It means* we have a God who was born for us, who died and rose for us, and then gave His Spirit so that we might continue to grow in wisdom and grace.

- *It means* we have a God who loves us enough to come to us as a Baby, placing Himself in our hands.

He loves us enough to give Himself away. He dares to make Himself vulnerable to us.

And so. . .

What do we dare?

MARIETTA DELLA PENNA

*H*e came down from Heaven" can almost be transposed into "Heaven drew earth up into it," and. . .limitation, sleep, sweat, footsore, weariness, frustration, pain, doubt, and death are. . .known by God from within. The pure light walks the earth; the darkness, received into the heart of the Deity, is there swallowed up.

C. S. LEWIS

If a poet or an artist puts himself into his Productions he is criticized. But that is exactly what God does, He does so in Christ. And precisely that is Christianity. The creation was really only completed when God included Himself in it. Before the coming of Christ, God was certainly in the creation, but as an invisible sign, like the watermark in paper. But the creation was completed by the Incarnation because God thereby included Himself in it.

Soren Kierkegaard

*The wonder of the Incarnation can
only be accepted with awe.
Jesus was wholly human,
and Jesus was wholly divine.
This is something that has baffled philosophers
and theologians for two thousand years.
Like love, it cannot be explained,
it can only be rejoiced in.*

MADELEINE L'ENGLE

Whence Comes this Rush of Wings?

Whence comes this rush of wings afar,
Following straight the Noel star?
Birds from the woods in wondrous flight,
Bethlehem seeks this Holy Night.

Angels and shepherds, birds of the sky,
Come where the Son of God doth lie;
Christ on earth with man doth dwell,
Join in the shout, "Noel, Noel!"

FRENCH CAROL FROM BAS-QUERCY

The world's perspective tells us to protect our rights. Common sense tells us not to take foolish risks, to think before we leap, to judge cautiously. We guard our hearts, protecting them from hurt, careful not give too much of ourselves away.

But at Christmas, Christ leaps to our earth, a Child with an unguarded heart who gives Himself completely. And in the end we hurt Him. In fact, we kill Him. He is foolish to come.

But the wisdom of Christmas has nothing to do with common sense.

Thank God.

The Holy Night

The magi of the East, in sandals worn,
Knelt reverent, sweeping round,
With long pale beards, their gifts upon
the ground,
The incense, myrrh, and gold
These baby hands were impotent to hold:
So let all earthlies and celestials wait
Upon thy royal state.
Sleep, sleep, my kingly One!

ELIZABETH BARRETT BROWNING

*D*ear Lord,

Thank You for loving us enough to be born a baby. You loved us enough to risk everything. Help us to love You enough to risk our hearts. Amen.

8

Echoes of Heaven:

A Time Beyond Time

December 25 comes only once a year. But Christmas is not limited to the calendar. Jesus can be born into our lives each day of the year, for His coming is eternal.

The big mistake we have made is to place it back there. *We have made it ancient history instead of modern life. It concerns angels, shepherds, Mary, Joseph and an innkeeper, but not us.*

We have decided, too, to confine Christmas to Christmas. On December twenty-fourth, it has not arrived ("Santa Claus does not come, Johnny, until tomorrow.") On December twenty-sixth, it is over ("We've got to get the tree outside, sweep the room, and clean up. It's all over, dear.")

So we don't really let Christmas come at all. By its very nature, it cannot be contained any more than God can be bottled up inside a church building to be visited once a week for an hour, or Jesus can be invoked in prayer to act as a convenient magician on call.

Fortunately, despite the fact that we don't let Christmas come at all, it is here all the time.

MALCOLM BOYD

$\mathcal{W}$*e are not finished with Christmas.*
To "serve its Founder's purpose,"
our celebrations must challenge us to explore,
to share, and to enjoy our Faith.

JOHN E. BAUR

The Lord Christ Jesu, God's son dear,
Was a guest and a stranger here;
Us for to bring from misery,
That we might live eternally.
All this did He for us freely,
For to declare His great mercy;
All Christendom be merry therefore,
And give Him thanks for evermore.

MILES COVERDALE

The wisdom that Christmas offers us—the rest and peace, the laughter and goodwill, the joy and love—all these give us a glimpse of something beyond our cloudy, humdrum world. The miracle and wonder of light on snow, of children singing "Away in a Manger" high and sweet, of gifts of love piled up around the tree—all these have a loveliness beyond themselves. They speak to us of something outside this world, something eternal. In them we see heaven's light, we hear angels' song, and we are piled high with God's bountiful grace.

The life of faith does not earn eternal life:
it is eternal life.
And Christ is its vehicle.

WILLIAM TEMPLE

As I decorate the tree each year at Christmas, tears often fill my eyes. I can't help but think of other Christmases, and the passage of time fills me with sadness. I remember being small at Christmas and the love my older sisters wrapped around me. I think of my brother who died so long ago; somehow each year at Christmas his absence seems sharp and new. As I hang a small ceramic heart on the tree, I long for the child it honors, a baby I miscarried on Christmas Eve five years ago.

Decorating the tree always reminds me of the passage of time. And I can't help but mourn for all that seems lost along the way.

But in reality, the glad light of Christmas never changes, no matter how many years go by. Christmas is the answer to our heartsick longing for all we have lost, for Christmas holds out a promise to us.

The name of that promise is eternity.

We know that the Son of God is come,
. . .that we may know him that is true,
and we are in him that is true,
even in his Son Jesus Christ.
This is the true God, and eternal life.

1 JOHN 5:20

This author heard echoes of eternity in the words "Once upon a time" from her childhood memories of Christmas. . . .

It was not merely because they were spoken with loving voices, the same voices that sang me to sleep and tucked me in with tender hands. . . . The depth of those fairy-tale words spoke to me of something true, kindled yearnings for a was-and-would be time, a kingdom I could almost remember but not name.

Christmas—and the days before and after—are celebrations of that yearning, our hearts' cry for fulfillment and peace. When we have lived long enough that earthly peace seems a mockery and promise another word for heartache, Christmas calls us to hope: for truth, beauty, holiness, and celebration.

EMILIE BARNES

At Christmas we think of the Baby—but that Baby is also our Savior—and He is also the King of Kings, who will reign for all eternity.

We think of Handel's *Messiah* as Christmas music—and it is. Yet it contains awesome images from Revelation, as this author comments. . . .

John in Revelation, and Handel, sum up all history in this one mysterious image. The great God who became a baby, who became a lamb, who became a sacrifice—this God, who bore our stripes and died our death, this one alone is worthy. That is where Handel leaves us, with the chorus "Worthy Is the Lamb," followed by exultant amens.

We were. . .in the late twentieth century in a materialistic culture light years removed from the imagery of slaughtered lambs. But Handel understood that history and civilization are not what they appear. [Dynasties,] civilizations—all rise and fall. History has proven beyond doubt that nothing fashioned by the hand of humanity will last. We need something greater than history, something outside history. We need a Lamb slain before the foundations of the world.

PHILIP YANCEY

I Sing the Birth

I sing the birth was born to-night,
The Author both of life and light;
The angels so did sound it.
And like the ravish'd shepherds said,
Who saw the light, and were afraid,
Yet search'd, and true they found it.

The Son of God, th' Eternal King,
That did us all salvation bring,
And freed the soul from danger;
He whom the whole world could not take,
The Word, which heaven and earth did make
Was now laid in a manger.

The Father's wisdom will'd it so,
The Son's obedience knew no No,
Both wills were in one stature;
And as that wisdom had decreed,
The Word was now made flesh indeed,
And took on Him our nature.

What comfort by Him do we win,
Who made Himself the price of sin,
To make us heirs of glory,
To see this Babe, all innocence;
A martyr born in our defence:
Can man forget this story?

BEN JONSON

*D*ear Lord,

Thank You for the wisdom of Christmas. Remind us to always keep in our hearts the gifts we find each year at this special time, gifts of homecoming and peace, hospitality and laughter, joy and love.

And, Lord, may our Christmases be more than seasonal celebrations. This year, show us the way to step beyond the pressures and constraints of our busy schedules. Help us to rest for just a moment in a place beyond time, listening to the echoes of heaven. Amen.

9

Christmas Wisdom:

Our Hearts' Desire

How far is it to Bethlehem?
Not very far.
Shall we find the stable-room
Lit by a star?

If we touch His tiny hand
Will He awake?
Will He know we've come so far
Just for His sake?

For all weary children
Mary must weep.
Here, on His bed of straw
Sleep, children, sleep.

God in His mother's arms,
Babes in the byre,
Sleep, as they sleep who find
Their heart's desire.

FRANCES CHESTERTON

How Far
to Bethlehem?

Sometimes the distance from our busy, complicated lives to that simple stable seems insurmountable. Our lives are filled with responsibilities and worries and longings—and the simple wisdom of Christmas is hard to grasp. In the end, though, if we follow the deepest desire of our hearts, we'll find ourselves kneeling beside the Baby's manger.

But our hearts' desire is not the same as the selfish cravings that distract us all. These are things that look good, but ultimately they fail to satisfy. Instead of leading us closer to God, they leave us anxious and restless, longing for something more. During December, most of us get distracted by cravings; after all, everywhere we look, we see holiday products and foods and experiences, each designed to stimulate our cravings.

We all get confused; we all make foolish mistakes. But the wisdom of Christmas still shines at the heart of our holiday celebrations. Quietly, simply, this wisdom points the way to our true hearts' desire: Jesus Christ.

The psychiatrist Gerald May says that "addiction exists wherever persons are internally compelled to give energy to things that are not true desires." Much of American consumerism panders to our addictions, rather than our desires. As we walk the malls with their abundance, we may be excited by the vast variety, but we may fill our carts with items which clutter our lives and dull the desires of our hearts.

PATRICK HOWELL

Infant holy, infant lowly,
For His bed a cattle stall;
Oxen lowing, little knowing,
Christ the babe is Lord of all.
Swift are winging angels singing,
Noels ringing, tidings bringing,
Christ the babe is Lord of all,
Christ the babe is Lord of all.

Flocks were sleeping, shepherds keeping,
Vigil till the morning new,
Saw the glory, heard the story,
Tidings of a gospel true.
Thus rejoicing, free from sorrow,
Praises voicing greet the morrow,
Christ the babe was born for you,
Christ the babe was born for you.

POLISH CAROL

Many merry Christmases,
friendships,
great accumulation of cheerful recollections,
affection on earth,
and Heaven at last for all of us.

CHARLES DICKENS

Christmas Prayer

O God, our loving Father,
help us rightly to remember the birth of Jesus,
that we may share in the song of the angels,
the gladness of the shepherds
and the worship of the wise men. . .
may the Christmas morning make us happy
to be Thy children
and the Christmas evening bring us to our beds
with grateful thoughts,
forgiving and forgiven, for Jesus' sake.
Amen.

ROBERT LOUIS STEVENSON

Merry
Christmas!